MEAT YOUR GOALS

YOUR LIFE IS AT STEAK!!?

Get it idiot!! God damn KENNY! I have to explain everything thing to you! GET YOUR SHIT TOGETHER!

BY: DICK HANDLER

MEAT YOUR GOALS
YOUR LIFE IS AT STEAK!!?

PUBLISHER: MEATY MEAT PRESS
WWW.MEATYOURGOALS.COM
ISBN 978-0-578-41695-3

Shit in this book:

Achnolwedge-me

'Bout Dick

The world is Fucked   1

Why the word is Fucked!   2

What the FUCK to do about it?   3

Why put MEAT at STEAK.. ?   10

The Environment? Ha! Like I care!   12

Furry things have feelings? Fuck that!   14

A Goal worth MEATING   17

FAT ASS GOALS FORMULA

     FUTURE-ISH   19

     AWESOMER   24

     TREACHEROUS   27

     ACTIONING   30

     SHAR-ED   31

     S....?   34

How to build a MEAT-UP group   46

When You Fail (You will, you failure!)   49

MEAT Kenny   50

MEAT LOG   64

Shit that's on my mind   86

BUY MY SHIT   88

Acknowledge-me

GOD DAMN! I AM FUCKING GREAT! You know it is true! SEE! You bought my crappy book!!

And this genius is all from me! I did this. We don't have no hand outs here!

That teacher lady in 6th grade who taught me how to read, I followed along! I made myself great! Fuck yeah!

I let all those other jackasses "help" me and I chose an ex-wife that would take care of the kids and bring in the money.

You are awesome Dick. I admire you!

To that old guy who was talking to me about writing this book, I bet you are expecting me to say something about you here.

NOPE. Write your damn own book! Quit hanging around "helping" people and fucking do something! You loser!

I mean really, look at me now. I got a fancy book and boy does it look good!

It's got pages and everything.

I want to acknowledge you Dick.

You did it.

DICK - THE ORIGINAL MEAT EATER FOR LIFE!! (TM)

'Bout Dick

Dick asked me to write about him.

He is okay. I like that he doesn't drink all the beer some times. I don't really understand what he says.

He blew it with his wife. Had a good thing going there.

I never had much to do with this whole "Make your life great" thing. But if that's your stuff, good on ya.

- Kenny

Fuck you dick!

You lazy ass. You have the ass to be the crapiest fucking father in the world and not work for years, then tell me you are some sort of guru and I should come to your weekly meeting to get my life sorted out!

You think I am the one you think needs to get sorted out? You are nuts!

Why don't you go sell your crazy shit to Kenny or your other idiot friends and pay some god damn child support. Your kids don't pay for themseleves!

- Dick's Ex-wife

MEAT YOUR GOALS (TM)

The world is FUCKED!

Dick here writing to you.

The world is fucked. You already know it is true. The world is fucked. There I said it again. And what happened to my truck!

WHAT THE FUCK HAPPENED TO MY TRUCK!
SHIT IS FUCKED!

How did it get this way? I was just going along and doing my own thing. Going with it. Then I wake up one morning, I have a shitty truck, I live in a dump, assface (the guy next door) throws his shit in my trash can and the wife and kids left.

WHAT THE FUCK!
THIS IS BULL SHIT.

I said "Dick, you are awesome, there must be something FUCKED with the world that is majorly fucking with your life. It is up to you to get that shit worked out and then profit off of teaching it to others, like that asshole Kenny down the street who always whining about some shit or another"
I listened. Dick knows his shit. I knew it was true.
So I started to look, and because I am a fucking genius, I figured that shit out. I know why the world is fucked, people!

1

Why the world is FUCKED!

It is fucked for one reason.
BECAUSE IT IS!
Yep. That is it.
Unsatisfied with that answer?
TOUGH. FUCKING. SHIT.

WHO GIVES A SHIT IF YOU ARE SATISFIED!?

You want to go around and see if you can figure it all out? See if you can find more people or bullshit to blame for your life being shitty? Want to feel good while you are drinking your god damn fancy coffee, sitting there in that fucking bullshit cafe down town, talking to that lame ass with the round glasses, about how you know what's going on in the world?

What a god damn joke...

You are just like "Lame Dick", the asshole I was my whole life until last week when I became a genius and was reborn a fuckin' "Meat Eater for Life"(TM). I was sitting there and bitching. I was a fucking bitch. Complaining about the wife taking my TV watching chair with her when she left with the kids. Spending time with that skinny ass loser Kenny. I admit it. I was a 'Grade A' whiny son of a god damned bitch.

I was gonna spend my whole god damn life that way. My tombstone would say: "Here Lies Dick. He Bitched about Everything." Fuck all of that.

WAKE UP FOLLOWER!!!

BUY MY SHIT!!!

Now, how did I become a genius and know what the fuck is up? Fuck you, I ain't gonna tell you shit. Buy my next book and hope that it is in there, you ungrateful asshole. Pissed that I am not going to tell you?

WELL TOUGH FUCKING SHIT. THE WORLD IS FUCKED. YOU BOUGHT THIS FUCKING BOOK AND THE ONE THING YOU WANTED, ISN'T IN IT.

TOUGH SHIT!

THE WORLD IS FUCKING FUCKED. GET THE FUCK OVER IT.

What the FUCK to do about it!

FUCK! I AM ON FIRE!

SHIT! Here's the real deal people. Ready for your life to change? Ready to finally figure out all the answers to all those pitiful questions you ask yourself while sitting in bed? How, oh how, can your miserable excuse for an existence get slightly less embarrassing?

Well FOLLOWER, you came to the right spot. At the right time! MY FIRST GENIUS HAPPENED TO ME LAST WEEK! No more "Whiny Dick"!

It was Friday nigh and I finished up pretending to give a shit about what that wuss of a boss man Jim was talking about and headed out to make fun of Kenny. Kenny wasn't at the bar, so I had both his drinks and mine. Then someone started playing Journey and it was over. That song's my song man! I love those guys. It was awesome! I was singin' and yelling and fucking doing it like the old times. Then the bastard bartender comes out of nowhere and throws me the out.

That guy pisses me off. Never go to Ted's bar downtown. I saw rats in the back. And Ted is a fucking dick.

After that bullshit, I headed home. This is where it got a bit fuzzy. I was walking by that new fangled gym at the fancy high school that our football team whooped last weekend. Then there was this door that was open and I went in and this jackass from some fancy ass city was talking.

Next thing I remember, I woke up on my front porch and I had this pamphlet about the "Meet Your Goals" formula in my hand.

It was a bunch of shitty city boy bull shit about this and that. They kept saying over and over that your life was at stake and if you didn't meet your goals you were destined to failure. And here I was, sitting there on the porch by the BBQ and that, FOLLOWER, was when my first genius struck.

It was like turning on a god damned light-bulb. It was just clear as that lake that I would push my little sister in when she was 3.

THOSE CITY FUCKS WERE IDIOTS!

IT IS NOT MEET YOUR GOALS!!

IT IS MEAT YOUR GOALS!! (TM)

It is god damned simple. Fuck even Kenny can get this.

What is worse that being a go damned city boy..? It is obvious... Not being a MEAT EATER!

FUCK! CAN YOU IMAGING NOT EATING MEAT FOR A WHOLE DAMN WEEK!

The MEAT YOUR GOALS FORMULA

1) Set a goal for the week.

2) If you don't MEAT it...You don't eat MEAT for the next week.

4

With that.. how is it even god damn possible to not reach your goals! This mean I won't have a shitty truck any more. This is genius! This would get anyone to do anything. Shit, I would even seal less from work if it meant I couldn't eat meat for a week.

And I came up with it! I am a genius. I came up with a whole Method for people to do great shit.

FUCK! I am fucking awesome! I need to drink more! I normally wake up in pool of piss. This time I woke up in a pile of genius!

It was so clear now! I could set weekly goals, and then make my life Fucking Great!

FUCK YOU SHITTY TRUCK!

I AM COMING FOR YOU, YOU BASTARD!

A MEAT EATTER FOR LIFE!!(TM) HAS BEEN BORN!

BUY MY SHIT!

So did you hear that follower? I will say it again for you. Here is my genius method that I created in the most productive black out of my life.

Meat Your Goal Formula:

Set a goal each week.

If you don't meet it, you can't eat meet for the next week. Repeat.

Isn't it fucking genius? I am a fucking genius! WHO IS A GENIUS? I AM! Dick Mother Fucking Handler!

Okay FOLLOWER, now you know why I am the leader and you are trailing 50 feet behind me picking up my shit and nodding when I say anything.

I am gonna tell you what the rest of this book is.

I know you are looking up at me and thinking "How can I be that guy?" Well news flash FOLLOWER, not possible. Your best hope is to be 1/4 the awesomer of me. Like if I was a six pack of tall boys, you would be the a half drunk can with a cigarette butt floating in it. Plus there is already one of me and with me being at the top, there isn't more room up here.

The rest of this book is to give you a glimmer of hope and show you how to use my Genius Meet Your Goals formula to regain some pieces of dignity.

I know it may be hard to believe. Even for you FOLLOWER, I am telling you it is possible for you to be slightly less of a fucking loser.

Look, Kenny at the corner store has been following me since high school and he is much less of a fuck up 30 years later.

If I can do that. Then I can do anything!

I am a genius!

I am a MEAT EATTER FOR LIFE!!

BUY MY SHIT!!!!

DRINK A SIX PACK AND COME BACK

YOU KNOW THAT WAS FUCKING GENIUS

ADMIT IT FOLLOWER!

READY FOR MORE?

OKAY LETS DO THIS!

Why put Meat at STEAK.. ?

SO YOU STILL ASKING THE BIG QUESTIONS?

HOW CAN I POSSIBLY NOT EAT MEAT FOR A WEEK?

Why not give up something easy like showering?

Well for starters, not eating meat is FUCKING EMBARRASSING!

The scene is set.
You and your friends are sitting at that round corner of Ronda's grill next to do the QuickStop.
Stephanie says to that crappy waiter boy: "I would love the T-Bone, rare as you wanna make it"
Impressed, waiter boy gives a nod and says "You know how to eat meat" with a smile.
Waiter boy turns to you and you stammer out some combination of grains and green things topped with a dairy product and look up embarrassed, silently asking for approval.
While waiter boy stands there staring at you in disbelief, Stephanie asks "Oh I didn't know you were vegetarian."
The moment you have dreaded has finally come to pass.

YOU ARE OFFICIALLY A GRADE "A" LOSER!

You mutter "No, what are you crazy! I just didn't Meat My Goals this week."
While you are glad you are not as much as an embarrassment as those god damn veg-people you still watch as Stephanie's disgust for you just keeps rising.
You are now one of them. You are a loser. Think about it,

how did you not MEAT YOUR GOALS this week. FUCK!

MEAT IS AWESOME!

That beautiful texture of a marbled rib-eye steak that has a thick burnt crust and an almost cold juicy center. There is nothing more delicious than that. Period. I hear those frenchies downtown at the fancy coffee place talking up things like cheese and wine or some other. They are so god damn wrong!

Eating meat is a FROM GOD!

It is our victory.

I AM A MEAT EATER FOR LIFE!(TM)

BUY MY SHIT!

...

YOU STILL COMPLAINING ABOUT PEOPLE EATING MEAT? WELL LET'S HERE IT THEN!

The Environment? Ha! Like I care!

There are all these new fangled smarty pant's out there who are sounding the dooms day bell saying thee world is ending. What a bunch of crap! I got to tell you, these liberal ass hats in these "Science" houses are such shit. I just looked on the computer and they just keep making shit up!

"Global Warming is the next threat to Humanity" they say.

If you are too hot, turn down the electric blanket!

"Global livestock contributes more 'green house' gases more than every car, plant, train and ship combined"

So? I have a green house in the backyard and it never hurt nobody. Oh and get this, they are really trying to stretch one out on us.

"65 percent of 'green house' gases are created from cows, sheep and goats belching and farting"

Well if that is a problem, teach them some damn manners and stop feeding them burritos! Hasn't your mama taught you right?
They even want to get all mathy on us and all that bull shit.

"30% of the earths surface is used to feed livestock for human consumption. While 10% is used for all other vegetables and grains that humans eat"

Great! You all stop eating Kale and add that 10% to the delicious meat pile! Mmmmm! Get in my belly!!!

"You need 48 times more water to produce the same amount of beef as veggies"

So what, I say! I got a creek in my back yard!

Then there are the damn America haters, who are really just jealous.

"Americans eat 122 kg (270 lb.) of meat a year on average, while Bangladeshis eat 1.8 kg (4 lb)."

Guess why everyone wants to wear the red, white and blue!

"The world could save a collective $730 bn in health care by reducing meat consumption"

What's a billion these days anyway! $730 bn is like 5 of those stupid I-Phone apps that the kids play with and one of those fancy doctor companies that is run by a damn liberal!

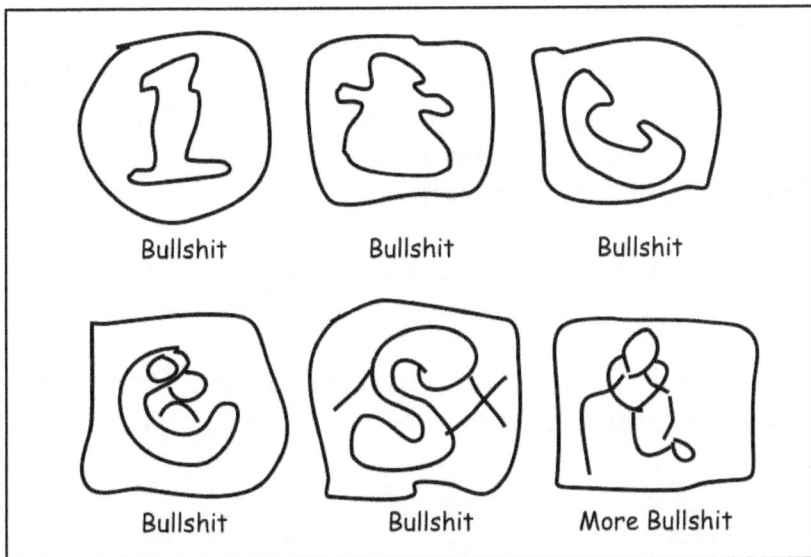

| Bullshit | Bullshit | Bullshit |
| Bullshit | Bullshit | More Bullshit |

ONE WORD! BULL SHIT!!!

Furry things have feelings?

Fuck that!

Oh god, puke!

Do you think that when the lions were chasing us back in the old days, that they were like "Oh that poor little thing that runs on two legs and has a really shitty fur coat... I really shouldn't eat it. That would hurt it. And it probably has a family."

FUCK NO!

Lions called our children by one name.. "DESERT!".

They be like, "I am gonna eat you.. then I am gonna eat you... then I am gonna take a nap.. then I am gonna eat THE REST OF YOU MOTHER FUCKERS!"

All these Lilly faces are so worried about how we are treating animals. IT IS SUCH BULLSHIT! I was on the computer the other day and clicking around and you will not believe all the crap they are saying.

"In egg factories, male chicks serve no purpose to the egg industry so they are ground up on the day they are born."

SO WHAT! Ever kicked out some jackass from a party to keep the "ratio" right? Yeah.. you know what I am talking about!

In terms of drugs, "more than 80 percent of antibiotics used in the US were used in Live Stock."

Big deal! All we have to do is travel south of the border to buy more! You don't even need a prescription! IT IS

AMAZING! YOU CAN GET THOSE BLUE MAN PILLS TOO! HA! But they keep coming with this BS.

"A US Dairy Cow has been genetically modified to product 10 times more milk than they would produce naturally."

THAT'S MA TALK'N 'BOUT! I will have two milkshakes then!

"82% of cows used for dairy production have their tails cut off."

So what! "Money Bags" Linda's fancy Boxer dog has its tail cut off. You going to go cry over that! GET OUT!

And those cry baby furry lovers are making movies about how all this MEAT making is bad! That some global conglomerate of business is "Bribing our elected officials" and what I eat!

WHAT A BUNCH OF NUT JOBS! I know all the people on the city council and I have been trying to bribe them for years with no god damn luck!

FUCK!

THAT IS A NEW GOAL!

BRIBE THE CITY COUNCIL!

YEAH! I GOT THIS!

I AM A MEAT EATER FOR LIFE!!(TM)

BUY MY SHIT!

A GOAL WORTH MEATING

Dick here writing to you.

Okay, let keep it real. Now you know why we are putting MEAT at STEAK!

On my genius night of discovery, I brought you one more thing, the solution to all of your problems: THE MEAT YOUR GOALS METHOD!!!

You no longer have to try all that bullshit that the science heads are talking about. Always giving you shit about eating this or that.

"DON'T EAT ALL THAT FAST FOOD OR YOU ARE GONNA GET DIABETES" THEY SAY. WHAT FUCKING HORSE SHIT. THOSE DOCTORS SITTING THERE TALKING LIKE THEY KNOW. THEY DON'T KNOW SHIT. I BEAT THE CRAP OUR OF OUR TOWN'S DOCTORS IN JUNIOR HIGH!

NOW FOLLOWER, YOU FINALLY HAVE THE TOOLS TO POWER!

What if you actually used them!? It could be fucking awesome!

Like the time that I jumped the motorbike across the creek. God damn! That fucking rocked. Kenny still talks about that. He still can't even believe it. It was great! Now, when I go to the quickstop, I get to sit there and hear people telling stories about me and all my greatness. I am awesome!!!

Now while you now have this awesomer method, unfortunately you are a still a damn loser. I know you are going to waist it's power on some bullshit and there is no god damn way that I am going to let that happen.

YOU ARE NOW MY FOLLOWER AND I AM GOING TO MAKE YOU A MEAT EATER FOR LIFE!!(TM)

Or if you suck, I will get rid of you faster than my first wife. Anyway FOLLOWER, it is time to get in this. Lets do this!

We need to start with getting you started. So lets start with something even an idiot like you can eek their way through.

What is your goal?

No, it okay, tell me....

Ha! Who am I kidding..I don't fucking care. You are just a brand new FOLLOWER.

Cute little baby FOLLOWER. Thinking you know what you are doing. Thinking you know how to set goals. How cute.

HAHAHAHAHAHA!!!!

Your goal are probably some bullshit that is marginally better than what you have now and so if you try for it you don't have to worry about failing. What a loser!

YOU THINK I GOT TO WHERE I AM TODAY BEING LIKE YOU. FUCK NO!

Is your goal like mine of jumping that bad ass 500cc metal beast across that glimmering stream? If you accomplished your goal would there be crowds cheering you? Would it be so awesome that your grand kids would tell their shitty friends at school about it?

Like 30 years from now your grand kid is on the playground

and is clearly a dork. So, your little dork is playing and some cool kids come up to them and say, "Hey Dork Suck, we are gonna kick your ass..!"

Then your kid's kid says, "Hey, I am from the Dork Suck family and we did cool shit, like (enter your goal here), so don't mess with me!"

Then the cool kids say, "Oh that's pretty cool... we ain't gonna mess with you!"

You see that is the power of a great goal. And while you really have no chance of achieving it like I do, because I am a Meat Eater for Life(TM), you maybe, just maybe, can do something cool enough that it keeps your grand kid from getting their butts whooped for a few extra god loving seconds.

So ask yourself: What could you that would be that awesome?

There is one way to do this, it is to follow my F.A.T. A.S.S. Goals Formula.

Your are right!

I have a god damn F.A.T. A.S.S. Goals formula!

I AM A GENIUS!! FOLLOW ME!!!

BUY MY SHIT!!!

LETS DO THIS!

AND LIKE ANY OF THOSE FANCY CITY BULL SHIT BOOKS, HERE ARE SOME LETTERS THAT SPELL SOMETHING THAT I WILL PRETEND MEAN SOMETHING!

HERE GOES YOUR MONEY!

F is for the Future-ish or some shit

(F.A.T. A.S.S. Goals)

Dick here writing to you.

This is some smart shit. Let's start with the first section of my F.A.T. Formula. F is for Future-ish. So, your goal needs to be in the Future-ISH! I told you it was some smart shit! Look at how my genius ass came up with it.

I was watching TV one night and this lady said some good stuff. And I know good shit when I see it. Like that time that Kenny was talking shit about how those Twinkies were 10 years old and was gonna throw them away. I was like "Hell No! Awesomer is for EVER" and I ate them. Man, were they fucking delicious.

Anyway, the lady in the TV said something about we just make small goals about how today could be better. Like, I want to get the earlier shift or have my doctor stop giving me bullshit about how much beer I drink. Fuck that guy!

She said that dumbasses like having small goals keeps them in the sucky life they are in. And guess who taught us ! Those damn teachers! THOSE JACKASSES ARE KEEPING US DOWN. THEY ARE FUCKING CONTROLLING US!

Then she said to have really bad ass goals we got to get really drunk or some shit and pretend we are in the future and we already got our goal done. Then see what the fuck actually mattered.

Like did it matter that I beat Jim to the last donut in the break room. You're god damn right it did. I showed him to not fuck with my last donut. Now, he knows not to race me and just takes the scraps after I am done. Jim is such a wuss!

But for you, look at all the shit you did in your life. You did all that and your life sucks. Look at your friends, they are fucking pathetic. So what the fuck was the point of all that shit you did?

If you died right now, would your Grand Kid tell their bullies about how cool you were.

Would they?

FUCK NO!

I mean, even I haven't even heard of you.

How big a deal could you be?

You ready to stop being a winer and be a LEVEL TWO FOLLOWER?

So, now get up and go to the mirror.

Don't make me fucking say it twice FOLLOWER!!

NOW!!!

Say the words out loud: "I am a loser who has made a bullshit life."

Then stare at yourself in the mirror.

Say it again!

"I am a loser who has made a bullshit life."

Now that we are on the same page, look deep in the mirror (this is the good stuff). Stare at that person like they were eyeballing you at the bar. Then use that messed up little head of yours to pretend it is 30 years from now and there is a little shit running around the playground somewhere, who is about to get their ass beat and your legacy is their only hope.

Say out loud in the trembling voice of a your future dorky fearful grand kid, "My Old person (you) was awesome, you should not kick my ass because they......"

Then just say things.

Say things until you say something that gets you fired the fuck up.

I mean really Fired the Fuck UP!!!

I MEAN TEAR THIS BOOK UP AND STOMP ON THE MOTHER FUCKING FLOOR FIRED UP!!!!!!!!!!

Like me, on last Saturday morning when I was sobering up. There I was, standing in front of the mirror saying shit.

I was envisioning my shitty grand kid being all alone on that bit of cement they call a play ground. The bullies run up to my grand kind and they are about to get pummeled. And my grand kid lets out a feeble...

"My old person was so awesome because they let Kenny hang with them, please don't kick my ass!"

I saw into the future, I could see my Grand Kid saying these words and the bullies looking at each other. They then smiled and said

"Kenny? Who the fuck is that? That supposed to scare us? Come here little shit, we are gonna pummel you!"

Then the ass beating commenced. Fuck!

I tried again because I am not a god damn quitter like you! I am a Meat Eater for Life(TM)! BUY MY SHIT!

"My Old person was so awesome, they .....didn't talk shit to their boss.. "

The beating came swiftly. (PS. See... fuck you Jim)

"...paid their child support on time.."

Beat down central!

"...Told the world it was fucked and made more money than your family is worth"

Oh, that got the little bullies attention. Well all of them besides the stupid one. He doesn't understand shit. But I was just getting started, you fucking future bullies trying to mess with my grand kid! I stared into the dirty mirror with my Ex's hair still in the drain and envisioned the future and said:

"My Old person was so awesome, they told the world it was fucked, made more money than your family is worth and now we own this shithole of a town"

Now the kids are looking at each other. I wanted more! I wanted to strike terror into their eyes. I went again!

"My Old person was so awesome, they told the world it was fucked, made more money than your family is worth and now we own this shithole of a town and if you fuck with me my family will pee in your fucking lemonade."

Now the kids are fucking running for the god damn hills. Fuck those kids!

See that is a god damn good goal.

My goals is to tell the world it is fucked, make so much money from it that I am gonna buy this shitty town and no one will be able to fuck with me or my Grand Kids.

FUCK YEAH! THAT F'N ROCKS!!

DO YOU FEEL IT FOLLOWER.
DO YOU FEEL THE POWER!

Now FOLLOWER, look in the mirror and say shit until you get fired the fuck up.

FIRED THE FUCK UP!!!

I AM A MEAT EATTER FOR LIFE! (TM)

BUY MY SHIT!

NOW YOU KNOW THE "F" STAGE OF F.A.T. A.S.S. GOALS!

MY GOAL THAT WILL SCARE THE SHIT OUT BULLIES WHO ARE ABOUT TO BEAT UP MY GRAND KIDS IS TO:

_____

_____

_____

_____

A is for Awesomer. Damn Right!

(F.A.T. A.S.S. Goals)

SO NOW WE ARE FIRED THE FUCK UP!!!

Fuck yes! This fucking rocks!

Okay now, we need to make a quick stop off...

Kenny... Kenny what the fuck! Kenny! Can you see that I am fucking writing here. I am in the middle of my fucking flow and you are fucking it up. If people don't like this book it is your god damn fault. Get the fuck off my front porch and don't come back here until I say so, you fucking ingrate. Where the hell you going. Leave the beer then get out. Yeah leave it right there. Okay now git you ass face outta here!

Okay, I am back with you now FOLLOWER, fucking Kenny, that shit, okay now where were we? Yes, we are gonna make a quick stop off in Awesomer town. This is the real shit. This is where we see if that bullshit you said to yourself in the mirror really fucking matters.

Like matters, not in a loser yelling at themselves in a mirror because a book told them to, kind of way. Like really fucking matters. Like it is on your fucking tombstone kind of way.

So this is the test. It is all high-tech as shit. Cause I am a genius. I know all about the tech shit. I use the interwebs and let googles do the bull shit for me.

Now FOLLOWERS, it is time to send some texts!

If you don't know how to text on a phone. Get one of those shitty kids next door that are always walking around with head phones on looking at their god damn shit bricks, to show you how to do it. It is called texting. Even though a fucking

24

phone is for talking, you have to touch these stupid ass little keys and write people fucking bullshit sentences.

When you get the hang of it, the next step is you have to text your "C.R.E.W." For those Jackasses who don't know what "C.R.E.W" means, I will make it fucking clear.

"C.R.E.W." = Crappy Relationships Everyone Wants

It is like all those people you are spending your time with but know you are better than. You know it is true FOLLOWER. Just look at your phone at all the people in it who you don't want to talk to. Those people are your C.R.E.W. Its like my ex-wifes brother. He was a fucking Patriots fan. Fuck man, I had to spend Thanks Giving with that asshat.

Okay, so you are going to text your "C.R.E.W" and tell them... you already completed your goal.

Yeah, be a god damned grown up and lie!

Don't worry it is good for you. Just text them each:

"I just ...... (Add your goal here)"

Then shut the fuck up and wait. This will be the ultimate test to see if you get to pass to the next level or if you are going to be a pathetic LEVEL 1 FOLLOWER FOR LIFE!(TM)

Okay, now that you have sent out the text messages you get to see if your Future-ish goals is AWESOMER!

If your lame ass C.R.E.W. respond with:

"No fucking way!!"
"Bullshit"
"Fuck you Dick!"
"You still owe me 8$ bucks you mother fucker"
"I have a restraining order on you! Don't text me!"

...then you know your goal is F'N AWESOMER!

YOU ARE NOW A LEVEL 2 FOLLOWER!!

If they respond with:

"Congratulations"
"Great"
"Good job"

Then your goal is not Awesomer and you are clearly fucking useless at reading this genius ass book. You need to sign up for one of my courses and sit in the back with the other BULL SHIT LEVEL ONE FOLLOWERS.

Once you have a verified Awesomer Goal, continue like the bad ass you are.

KENNY I FUCKING SEE YOU. YOUR GOAL SUCKS! GO BACK TO THE START! DON'T TRY TO FUCK WITH ME!

I AM A MEAT EATTER FOR LIFE(TM)!!

BUY MY SHIT!

T is for Treacherous. Spelled it right!

How you like that!

(F.A.T. A.S.S. Goals)

Dick here writing to you.

I added Treacherous for you. Yep you. The piece of shit with the bullshit hat that was fooling nobody, that showed up to my event last night and then left, pretending they got the "wrong room". I see you joker! That fear you are running from, well it is what is messing up your life!

You need to be afraid of your goals.

Also.. Kenny.. next time you are hosting me at your house, stop fucking eating all the god damn cookies. That was some bull shit. How am I gonna get these people to give me all their moneys if there ain't no damn free cookies. I don't care if your mom made them or not. Stop eating them!

Okay, back to it. Yeah, you need to be afraid of your goals. I mean I have no fucking clue what being a scared wussy is like, because I am fucking AWESOME!

I AM A MEAT EATTER FOR LIFE!(TM)

BUY MY SHIT!

But you, you know the feeling. That time when you heard a loud sound in the dark in your basement and you jumped.

Or that time in gym class when you looked up at the rope hanging from the ceiling and were afraid to climb it. Or when you knew the cool kids were partying in the woods and you were too afraid to sneak out and be a bad ass?

Yeah that feeling. You know it. I can smell it on you.

I am going to show you how to take that feeling and crush it, then take the dust and build an endless inferno of the will to win. Fuck yeah!

I AM FIRING MY SHIT UP!

Okay, so if you are a LOSER, like you there reading this right now, if your goal is not scaring the shit out of you, you are either either pathetic or full of BS. You big dummy.

If you are aiming not big enough, when you think of your goal you will see yourself saying "ehh".

Oh, right I forgot, they don't teach "Ehh" in reject school. Let me fill you in. It's like how you feel about being nice to the neighbor down the street. You could but "...Ehh".

Like you could tell Jim, your boss, that he has toilet paper coming out his pants when he walks by but "...Ehh".

Or you could tell Kenny that he is about to walk into that ladder, but "...Ehh".

Next, if your goal is too big, you say some shit like "Sure thats my goal but the fucks the point." God damn, nothing pisses me off more. There you go, fucking quiting without even starting.

What a fucking lame-ass..

The best way to check if your goals is treacherous or not, is when you say it to someone, your hands get all sweaty. Like when the plumber comes over and it is hot as shit, and he is fixing shit and you see down is ass crack. That kind of sweaty.

So, the moral of the story is to make sure that your goal

is Treacherous or for some asshats like Kenny who both interrupts me and didn't make it past 6th grade, scary.

Get it Kenny?! Treacherous means scary! You idjit!

God damn. What is something treacherous, its like that time I hooked up with Kenny's sister and Kenny almost found out!

(Ha! Ha! Fuck you Kenny, you shouldn't have come over while I was writing. Next time when I tell you to get beer, just leave it on the god damned porch and go home!)

More real talk

Dick here writing to you.

Okay FOLLOWER, I have now shown you how to select what type of goals to have. They should be set Future-ish goals and be both Awesomer and Treacherous.

Now, I know quitters like you can take this genius and fucking squander it and return to your couch only to rise to shit and complain. To save you from that inevitable fate, I GOT SOME A.S.S. FOR YOU!

I AM GOING TO GIVE YOU THE REAL TALK!

I AM ON A ROLL!

I AM A MEAT EATER FOR LIFE (TM)

BUY MY SHIT!!

29

Making Goals Real as Fuck!

Okay, newsflash, I am gonna tell you real quick. My first goal was to make out with Stacy. She was the hottest girl in third grade. In high school when we graduated, and she moved away. My chance was over.

(STACY I KNOW YOU ARE READING THIS!)

I didn't have my genius "Meat You Goals" formula then. So, I, like you, failed. Why am I telling you this? Because it is the secret to my greatness.

(STACY, HOW YOU LIKE MY BOOK. BET YOU WANT TO DITCH THAT FUCKWAD AND GET WITH ME NOW! WELL YOU CAN'T! HA! I AM OVER YOUR ASS)

Me failing like a god damned failure with Stacy, was some real bullshit. I am almost over it. It was also the seed of my Genius!

(STACY IF YOU ARE STILL HOT, EMAIL ME AT RHANDLER62@AOL.COM)

It is how I invented the second half of the F.A.T. A.S.S. Goals method.

Goals need to be:

ACTIONING:

To be honest I was checking out Stacy when they told us what this word meant so, fuck if I know. It think it has to do with some bullshit about doing things. It is like some fancy as way of saying, Do-able.

So for all you rejects out there I put this in, your goals need to be Do-Able. Like you can see them actually happening. Not something like you saying "I want to be like DICK THE GENIUS and write a genius books like this."

But more like, I want to go to see Dick at his next motivational speaker tour and pay all the money so I can drink a beer with him and have him yell at me.

Like that. The main reason I failed with Stacy, is that I wasn't aiming high enough. She wasn't do-able. I was way out of her league. So you got to be straight with yourself. Look at all of your uglies and choose something that your pathetic self can actually do.

Like, subscribing to my newsletter or wearing a "I Meat My Goals" T-shirt for a week.

GET IT?

I AM TELLING YOU TO SIGN UP FOR MY MAILING LIST!

DID YOU SIGN UP FOR MY MAILING LIST?

DON'T MESS WITH ME!

I AM A MEAT EATER FOR LIFE!(TM)

DID YOU SIGN UP FOR MY MAILING LIST? OKAY? GOOD. Moving on.

SHAR-ED:

Next, your goals need to be Shar-ed. You got to tell people about them. Like I wrote "Dick Sucks Stacey" on the 3rd stall to the right in the bathroom. I thought that was shar-ed but that clearly wasn't enough now was it?

Like which Dick was it? Which Stacy? How do I know people actually read it? Did Stacy ever go into the boys bathroom? You have to yell what you want for the roof tops!!

Here's how a BAD ASS does it!

STACY IF YOU ARE STILL HOT, IT IS MY GOAL TO HAVE YOU ACCEPT MY FRIEND REQUEST ON THE FACE BOOKS.

STACY!! ACCEPT MY GOD DAMNED FRIEND REQUEST!

You really have to share what you want with everyone.

Like Frank at the corner store knows all about how I want Stacy to accept my friend my request and like my posts. It will be awesomer as then my other ex's will be jealous. And the important part of it is that now, Frank talks to me about my goal! Yesterday, when I stopped by for a pack, Frank said "Hey, 'sup with you and that Stacy lady?"

So it keeps the goal alive, not that I need that help as I am a "Meat Eater For Life" (TM). But FOLLOWER, you for sure need it. How would you possibly perform at my level without intense social pressure from those lame people hanging around you?

YOU ARE RIGHT YOU COULDN'T.

SO SHARE YOUR GOALS!

If someone like Jim at work is talking about some shit he did with his kids last weekend, just interrupt and let him know what's up.

Jim: "....so after we got Mary out of intensive care and her grandma brought her this really cute bear and LEGO set.."

Dick: "Dave SHUT UP! WHERE WERE YOU FRIDAY NIGHT? You need to come to my 'Meat Your Goals' launch night on Friday, bring your whinny girl and you mom. It's my goal to have 13 people there. You 3 and you friends would at least count for something until the non-fuckups arrive."

You see FOLLOWER? I told him my goal.

Did I wait for him to finish talking about whatever he was talking about..?

FUCK NO!

I GOT GOALS!

I NEED TO SHARE THEM

I AM A MEAT EATER FOR LIFE!!(TM)

BUY MY SHIT!

NOW ONTO THE NEXT GENIUS PART!

THE LAST STAGE OF F.A.T. A.S.S GOALS, STARTS WITH AN S....

SHAR-ED (AGAIN):

IT IS SHAR-ED (AGAIN)!! YES YOU BOUGHT A BOOK THAT USED THE SAME ITEM TWICE!

STOP YOUR DAMN WHINING!

GENIUS IS ABOUT YOU HIT YOU IN THE FACE LIKE STEAK WHILE STANDING IN A FOOTBALL FIELD.

KENNY, DON'T BE LATE FOR MEATINGS, IF YOU DON'T WANT TO GET SLAPPED!

I know, you are saying didn't we just share our goals?

That is the genius of it and it is where quitters like you fail. It is the reason why you are reading my book and I am sitting back making money off your inability to do any thing remotely impressive with your life.

You have to share your goals again!
But this time, like a rabid wombat that likes the taste of human. Here, learn from the master.

YOU WILL LEARN FROM ME!!!

I AM A MEAT EATER FOR LIFE!!(TM)

I went in early to work on Sunday as I am a bad ass.
I went to the copier machine at work and made 100 copies of my "Meat Your Goals" event flier. Note: I saved money by using work's paper and ink. Jim the office manager is a joker, always being a dick and asking me to do shit. If his dad didn't

run the place I would give him a grade "A" ass whoopin!

YOU HEAR ME JIM!

Anyway, after making the copies, I put one in each drawer of Dave, Sarah's, Jerome's and "Lame Matt's" desks.
Then, brilliant me put the extras upside down in the place where you add paper to the printer, HA!

Bet you never heard that one before!

I AM A FUCKING GENIUS.

Now, whenever someone prints something out, on the back of their bull shit reports, will be all the information people need to attend my event!
I told you I am a genius! Now, everyone will know about it!

Fuck it, I will put it here.

It's this FRIDAY night at Hilda's in the back right. Look for me in my Awesomer purple "Meat Eater for Life"!!(TM) jacket.

See that is how a genius works people!

SHARE MY SHIT!

COME TO MY EVENT!

I AM A MEAT EATER FOR LIFE!! (TM)

BUY MY SHIT!!!!

Okay Now shit gets real!!

Before you move forward, it's your time you shit stain!!

Set your first weekly goal! DO IT NOW!

DO IT NOW!!

WHAT ARE YOU DOING!!! GO BACK AND SET A DAMN GOAL!

KENNY I AM GOD DAMN SERIOUS!

SHIT IS GONNA GET REAL!

DID YOU SET THE GOAL?

IF YES:

MOVE ON SLOW POKE!

IF NO:

GAME OVER! I AM COMING FOR YOU KENNY!

GREAT ANY IDIOT CAN SET A GOAL!

NOW, GO GET YOU GOAL DONE.

WHAT DOES IT DAMN MATTER IF YOU READ THIS BOOK, IF YOU DON'T DO YOUR SHIT!

KENNY I AM FUCKING SERIOUS

OKAY, YOU BACK?

SWEET.

LETS DO THIS!

Did you MEAT Your Goals?

IF YES:

I AM WATCHING YOU KENNY!
I AM RIGHT BEHIND YOU.
YOU ARE LYING YOU LIE FACE!!
TAKE A GOD DAMED SHOWER!!!

IF YOU ARE NOT KENNY, CONTINUE ON. YOU ARE NOW A TIER 3 FOLLOWER.

IF NO!

FUCK! I KNEW IT! You are not like me!

I AM A MEAT EATER FOR LIFE!!(TM)

This is why your life is like it is. You half ass it. Sure you say "I am better than this jackass writing this book, I do want I want!" Here some genius for you. Who else don't you listen to. Ever wonder why you life is fucked! That's it!

CLOSE THIS BOOK AND GO MEAT YOUR GOALS!

How to build a MEAT-UP group

Now you are setting goals and MEATING them, you now get to move on to the next level.

YOU GET TO HAVE YOUR OWN FOLLOWERS!!

YOU CAN MAYBE BE BARELY AS AWESOME AS ME!

Okay, here is how you do it. Real talk time. Listen up!

To start, tell all your "C.R.E.W." that you're are having a party at the parking log behind your house. Tell them that you are smoking a brisket, BBQ'ing a rack of ribs and just picked up some Rib-eyes. Ask them to pitch in $18 bucks for the meat up front! None of this "Ill pay you later" bullshit.

Once you get the money, go to "MeatYourGoals.com" and buy a book for each of those suckers. Have it mailed to your house.

You can keep the couple of bucks change. You are welcome.

And, next time order more books. I am watching. I ship every last one of those mother fuckers. I know how many FOLLOWERS you have!

How do you think you get to FOLLOWER 4 status?

Okay back to the goals:

Then on the night of the big event gather all the guests in front of your house, there should be at least 10 of them.

Once gathered, ask: "Who's life is so fucking good that they can't believe it? Where all aspects of your life are amazing. If that is true for you, raising your hand?"

As you know, unless they have read this book and become a Meat Eater for Life!!(TM), having a life you love is not possible.

If you have gotten this far into the book and are just realizing this, you are stupider than I look.

Ha!

Now back to your front yard. If anyone raises their hand, keep asking them question about parts of their life. Find something that sucks or is not as good as they would want it to be.

If they keep their hand raise say "Well you know what doesn't work, is you coming here and lying to all your friends in my house! Get the fuck out!"

Then keep yelling at them until they leave.

LIKE FUCKING KENNY! YOU LIVE WITH YOUR MOM KENNY! YOUR LIFE SUCKS!! PUT YOUR HAND DOWN!!

Okay, after everyone has admitted that they have a fucked up life and the liars have been removed, move on to the next question.

"Who of you set goals for the past week? If you have set goals raise your hand."

Next for those who set goals, ask "Who of you achieved 100% of those goals? If you have, keep your hand raised."

If any of them fakers still have their hands raised, stare at them with the fire of a thousand suns until they realized the errors of their ways and timidly lower their hands.

Note: If you are un-successful at this, call me at the bar so I can give you the biggest raft of shit in your life.

Now you have them. It is time to close.

"Okay so I have called you here for a wake up call. Your lives suck and you are doing not a fucking damn thing about it. I could have been your sucky friend and used your money to buy great steaks for you, but you are fucking up your lives. So you don't deserve MEAT. This is an intervention mother fuckers! It is time to MEAT YOUR GOALS."

NOW, TAKE THE BOOKS FROM YOUR STUDDED BACKPACK AND START THROWING THEM AT THESE COWARDS. IF ANY OF THEM ARE CLOSE ENOUGH, SLAP THEM IN THE FACE WITH THE BOOKS!

Then continue, "Read it, live by it, it is your second bible! You are now on the path to being like me a 'MEAT EATER FOR LIFE'(TM)"

Then stare at them and keep repeat it while yelling over their voices if they ask any questions. If you need to slap more of them, do it.

DO IT FOLLOWER!

Half of them will leave. Those are the QUITTERS. They will see the light later and come crawling back like that time when Kenny crashed Frank's car and then came back and Frank gave him an ass whooping.

The rest that stay are your first FOLLOWERS and your MEAT-UP GROUP!.

They are now your followers. You have to make them "MEAT EATERS FOR LIFE"!!(TM). If you don't, I am gonna know about it. Bring them to my Friday event next week!

SEE FOLLOWER!

YOU ARE NOT AS SHITTY AS YOU THOUGHT!

YOU FOLLOWED ME AND I SHOWED YOU THE WAY

WE ARE MEAT EATERS FOR LIFE!!(TM)

BUY MY SHIT!

When You Fail (You will, you failure!)

IT IS CLEAR!!

I CAN SEE IT EASILY! YOU HAVE FAILED BECAUSE YOU HAVE NOT PURCHASED ENOUGH OF MY SHIT!

BUY IT! NOW!!

NO KENNY NONE OF THIS I.O.U. STUFF!!!

AND WHAT KIND OF GROWN ASS MAN SAYS HIS MOM WILL PAY FOR IT!!

WHAT THE FUCK KENNY??!!!

BUY MY SHIT!!!

BUY IT!!!

MEAT KENNY

Dick here writing to you.

FOLLOWERS, here is the deal, when I am drunk and I yell at my computer it somehow knows what I am thinking. Shit is fucking crazy! I fought it at first and was gonna go beat the shit out of those techies who did this to me.. but then I sobered up and read what it wrote and I was like "Hey this is some genius right here. You should keep this going Dick! Now the whole world can see the awesomer stuff in your head!"

So world, WELCOME TO THE HEAD OF A MEAT EATTER FOR LIFE!

BUY MY SHIT!

TUESDAY 6 WEEKS AGO

Look there's Kenny again. What a god damn loser. There he is just shuffling along. He walks so damn slow. I hate walking slow. I got places to be. I am important as SHIT!

Wonder what he is doing. This lame ass is going to be the perfect specimen for my method of greatness! I will make him Meat His Goals, or at least pretend to and the tell big lies about it, and then I will make millions off of using his shit stain of a life to prove my method works. It's like shooting fish in a fucking barrel. His life is so shit I could do anything and it would be better.

Okay, Dick let's do this. Are you a MEAT EATER FOR LIFE!!(TM) Dick!!?? Are you!!?

THEN GO DO IT!

"KENNY!"

That asshole never hears me

"KENNY!!"

Fucking finally!

"..hey.."

"WHAT DO YOU MEAN HEY?!! TODAY IS YOUR DAY. IT'S FRIDAY. LET'S GET FIRED UP!"

I can't believe that I have to work with this sorry sack.

"..okay, you talkin' about me eating meat again?"

"NO KENNY, GOD DAMN IT! NO. THAT WAS LAST WEEK, THIS IS TOTALLY DIFFERENT. I CAN'T BELIEVE YOU KENNY. NOW HERE IS THE DEAL. YOU ARE GONNA SET A GOAL AND IF YOU DON'T MEAT IT, THEN YOU AREN'T GONNA BE ABLE TO EAT MEAT NEXT WEEK"

"...ahh.. that's what you said last..."

"SHUT THE FUCK UP KENNY!"

"...I got to go.. my mama needs her pills"

"GOD DAMN IT. THIS IS TOTALLY DIFFERENT. LAST WEEK I HADN'T INVENTED MY GENIUS F.A.T. A.S.S. METHOD? NOW WHAT IS YOUR GOAL FOR FRIDAY!"

"Ah.. I guess I would like to get me a lady.."

Ha a fucking lady? This loser. What a jackass. I can't believe I need to use his ass for my book. Okay, now I got to fire him up.

"THERE WE GO KENNY, HOW DAMN HARD WAS THAT?

"..not bad..."

51

"OKAY HOW ARE YOU GONNA DO THAT. WHAT ARE YOU GONNA DO TO MAKE THAT HAPPEN?"

"..ask ..ask my mom, if I could go out on Thursday?"

"GREAT KENNY. THAT IS IT. THAT IS IT. FUCK YEAH!"

"okay.... can I go now..."

"NOW REMEMBER. GET YOU MOM TO COME FRIDAY!"

"yea.. I will tell her about your meeting next week..."

"DAMN STRAIGHT!"

Phew, god damn. Fuck. Okay Dick, you got to keep going. You are awesome. You are sooo awesome!! This method is genius. You will show'em. You are a Meat Eater for Life!! (TM). Now let's get a beer to celebrate! Fuck yeah!

The Next Friday

Okay, where the hell is Kenny? I have been watching this damn road for since noon and I know he hasn't walked home yet. It was totally worth it to piss in the bucket, so I didn't have to leave the porch. I am a bad ass! This is gonna look so damn good when I tell about it at my sweet event on Friday!

I bet that asshat took the alley back to his mom's house to get away from me. THINK YOU ARE SO DAMN SMART KENNY! I AM COMING FOR YOU!!

Okay where is his house again..? God damn I hate walking. Should have taken the truck. Okay, is that the one? Oh yeah, thats the one. That is the cat that Kenny keeps showing me pictures of when I am talking over him.

Knock Knock

......

Knock Knock

"KENNY!! YOUR ASS GET OUT HERE!!"

Knock Knock

......

"hello? Who's that?"

"MY APOLOGIES MAM' THIS IS DICK FROM DOWN THE STREET. CAN YOU HEAR ME OKAY? I AM HERE FOR YOUR SON KENNY."

"Are you the one with the meetings..?"

"YES MAM"

"Hmmm... okay Kenny is in the back playing his games.."

Ahhh hell no! He is avoiding me. Okay Dick, time to get all up in his face. Think about the future when you are getting pumped up back stage to go out to huge applause from all your FOLLOWERS. It is going to be amazing. They are going to yell and throw things in the air and then shut the fuck up when you tell them to. It is going to be down right magical. Okay, so you know the drill, go into those deep dark depths of this hovel and get that man on track!

"MIND IF I GO IN MAM'?"

"..'suppose so...."

God damn it is creepy in here... but it is pretty darn clean... Maybe I should live with my mama, Kenny has got it pretty good thing goin' here. I mean it is a fucking disgrace but shit, it is a clean disgrace! Okay Dick get your head in the damn game son. This shit is for real. You got this! You are a god damn

MEAT EATER FOR LIFE!!(TM) Fucking go for it!!! That's his door, I can see the fucking loser video game lights from the TV under the door. You need a damn good entrance! Like it is going to be on TV when you have your own show. This is your signature move, just bust in like a that guy in those movies back in the day"

BOOOM! (THE DOOR CRASHES UNDER DICK'S BOOT)

"FUCKIN' KENNY!!! IT IS FRIDAY DID YOU MEAT YOUR GOALS!!!"

"...b.. but.. Dick... what... you just broke down my door... what are you doing here...?"

"DID YOU OR DID YOU NOT MEAT YOUR GOALS MOTHER FUCKER!!???"

"...stop ...stop yelling.. Dick you are scaring me..."

"DID YOU OR DIDN'T YOU MEAT YOUR FUCKING GOALS!!! ANSWER ME!!!"

"....what...? ... my goals"

"GOD DAMMIT KENNY, YOUR GOALS FOR THE WEEK WERE TO GO OUT ON THURSDAY NIGHT AND MEET A LADY!!! DID YOU DO IT??!!!"

"..what?...you don't have to stand so close to me and talk so loud... yeah... I remember... I did my goal... ... my Mama said no..."

"WHAT? THAT WASN'T YOUR GOAL! YOUR GOAL WAS TO GO OUT!"

"... I don't know.... I think it was to ask my Mama if I could go out... yeah remember you were standing there on the sidewalk when I was walking home... and then we talked and I said my goal was to ask my Mama....?"

"FUCK YOU KENNY! YOU ARE FUCKING THIS UP!"

"....what?...dick what did I do..?.... I asked her and she said no. She had her shows that night and said I needed to help her record them.... so I did it.... does that mean I am a Meat Eater Like you!?"

"FUCK! NO! GOD DAMN KENNY! ONLY YOU COULD TAKE THE GENIUS F.A.T. A.S.S. GOAL SETTING METHOD AND GO AND TOTALLY FUCK IT UP! LOOK AT YOU. YOU ARE JUST SITTING HERE AND DOING THE SAME GOD DAMN SHIT YOU HAVE BEEN FOR YEARS AND YOU THINK YOU ARE FUCKING MEAT EATER FOR LIFE!!(TM) FUCK YOU!"

..whoa Dick.. you got to bring it back in. You are losing him. He looks like he is about to cry like a little wussy. If he cries there is no way his mom is coming to the MEAT-UP on Friday. You got to deal with some bullshit and make this kid a damn man!

"OKAY, SO LETS AGREE THAT YOU ARE A MAJOR FUCK UP, YOU FAILED YOUR FIRST GOAL AND IT WAS ALL YOUR FAULT FOR MAKING UP SHITTY GOALS. SO, NO MORE SHITTY GOALS KENNY. THEY HAVE TO BE SOMETHING THAT IS ABOUT SOME GOD DAMNED RESULTS. DO YOU UNDERSTAND? NOT SOME DAMN 'I AM GONNA ASK MY MAMA SOMETHING....' THEY ARE GONNA BE BIG SHIT. LIKE THINGS THAT IF THEY HAPPENED WOULD REALLY MATTER! DO YOU HEAR ME..!!!?"

"...okay Dick... I don't know why you need to get in my face about it..."

"KENNY. I HAVE TO GET IN YOUR GOD DAMNED FACE BECAUSE YOUR LIFE FUCKING MATTERS!!!"

THIS IS GOING TO BE SO GOOD WHEN I TELL PEOPLE

ABOUT IT LATER. DICK YOU ARE NAILING IT! THIS IS GOING TO BE ONE OF THE STORIES EVERYONE TELLS ABOUT YOU WHEN YOU ARE UP THERE IN FRONT THE COLISEUM AND THE MAYOR IS GIVING YOU THE MOTHERFUCKING KEYS TO THE CITY! THIS IS GOING TO BE AWESOME

"..okay Dick... what should I do now?"

"EASY! IT IS TIME FOR SOME F.A.T. A.S.S. GOALS! LETS START WITH LOOKING FROM THE FUTURE BACK TO NOW. LOOK WAY AHEAD AND IMAGINE YOURSELF 5 YEARS FROM NOW AND YOUR GOALS ARE ALREADY NAILED. CLOSE YOUR EYES AND THINK.. WHAT IS IT LIKE IN 5 YEARS"

"..okay... it is five years from now... I am playing video games in this house.. my mom is there..."

"GOD DAMN IT KENNY! THAT IS THE SAME AS TODAY! OKAY YOU NEED TO MAKE YOUR GOALS AWESOMER. WHAT IF TRUE IN 5 YEARS WOULD BE AWESOMER? SO AWESOMER, THAT YOUR KIDS.. OR IN YOUR CASE.... YOUR CAT, IN THE FUTURE WHEN YOU ARE GONE.. WOULD NOT GET MESSED WITH BECAUSE WHAT YOU DID WAS SO AWESOMER!!"

"..but my cat is old Dick... I don't think he is going to live much longer..."

"FUCK KENNY. GOD DAMNED IT! PRETEND YOU HAVE KIDS OR A CAT THAT LIVES FOR EVER!"

"..okay, it's 5 years from now and I did something that is awesomer... so awesomer that my Kids or Cat will not get messed with because it is so awesome..."

"...my kids... ...I have a kid... I HAVE A KID!.... DICK IN 5 YEARS I HAVE A KID!!!"

"WOAH KENNY, I DIDN'T SAY THAT!!! LET'S CALM IT DOWN"

"NO! I SAW IT DICK. I SAW HER. I SAW HER DICK! I HAVE A KID IN 5 YEARS! DICK YOU GAVE ME A KID! THIS IS FUCKING BEAUTIFUL."

"AHH YEAH.. OKAY... WELL DOES IT ALSO FEEL TREACHEROUS?"

"YES! I AM TERRIFIED DICK!"

FUCK DICK. YOUR POWERS ARE TOO STRONG. I HAVE NEVER SEEN KENNY LIKE THIS BEFORE. I THINK THIS IS HOW AWESOMER YOU ARE DICK. YOU ARE GOING TO MAKE PEOPLE LOSE THEIR MINDS. YOU GOT TO PRETEND THAT YOU KNEW THIS WAS GOING TO HAPPEN. THIS IS YOUR MOMENT DICK. DON'T BLOW IT.

"OKAY.. NOW... GOOD.... YOU GOT THE F.A.T. PART. WHAT ABOUT THE A.S.S. PART? WHAT IS YOUR ACTIONING GOAL FOR THIS WEEK?"

"GREAT QUESTION DICK. I GUESS I NEED TO TAKE ACTION TO GO OUT THERE AN FIND MY GAL. I AM GOING TO GO OUT EVERY NIGHT! THIS IS GOING TO BE AMAZING. I AM SO TERRIFIED DICK!"

"SHUT THAT DAMN TRAP! NONE OF THIS TERRIFIED CRAP. REMEMBER WHEN YOU SAW YOUR KID. THAT IS ALL THAT MATTERS NOW. SO SHUT IT AND GET SOME ACTIONING UNDER YOUR BELT!"

THERE YOU GO DICK. YOU ARE BACK IN THE SADDLE. LET'S BRING THIS HOME.

"YOU ARE RIGHT DICK! I AM SO SORRY FOR NOT BELIEVING IN YOU EARLIER... THIS IS AMAZING! I AM GOING TO BE A DAD!"

"OKAY GOOD KENNY.. THE NEXT A.S.S. STEP IS TO SHARE IT. SO WHO CAN YOU TELL ABOUT IT?"

"MOM! MOM!! MOM! WHERE ARE YOU?"

OH LOOK THERE HE GOES, RUNNING AROUND LOOKING FOR THAT OLD BAG. OKAY DICK PRETEND YOU ARE INTERESTED AND GO FOLLOW HIM. YOU GOT TO CLOSE THIS SO YOU CAN TELL PEOPLE ABOUT IT LATER.

"MOM! I HAVE TO TELL YOU SOMETHING!!!"

"...what... I am watching my shows son.... ..why have you been spending time with that friend of yours again..?"

"MOM DICK SAVED ME!! I JUST SAW IT. IN 5 YEARS I AM GOING TO HAVE A KID! I AM GOING TO HAVE A BOY MOM! YOU ARE GOING TO BE A GRANDMA!"

"...what.. you have never been with a girl son... ...what are you talking about... did Dick put you up to this...?

"NO! HE HELPED ME SEE! I AM GOING TO GO OUT AND MEET MY WIFE THIS WEEK! I AM GOING TO BE A DAD!"

"..okay son...okay..my show is starting..."

NOW IT IS TIME TO REALLY GET HIM TO BE USEFUL TO YOU DICK. THOSE FOLLOWERS WON'T GROW THEMSELVES!

"OKAY KENNY AND KENNY MOM! YOU HAVE SEEN THE POWER! KENNY YOU HAVE YOUR GOALS FOR THE WEEK. I EXPECT YOU TO GET THEM DONE AND THEN BE AT MY PLACE ON FRIDAY AT 5PM WITH YOUR WIFE."

"YES DICK! YES!"

OKAY DICK, LET'S GET THE FUCK OUT OF HERE. KENNY LOOKS LIKE THAT GUY DOWN TOWN WHO COOKS DRUGS IN THE HOTEL.

THE NEXT FRIDAY

GOD DAMN. KENNY IS COMING OVER FOR THE MEETING TONIGHT... I HOPE THAT LAME ASS DOESN'T SHOW, SO I CAN GO OVER AND GIVE HIM A GOOD YELLING AT AGAIN. YELLIN' AT HIM IS SO FUN!

OKAY DICK. THIS IS YOUR FIRST FOLLOWER. YOU HAVE TO MAKE THIS WORK. REMEMBER LAST TIME WITH JED. YOU DON'T WANT TO DO THAT AGAIN. THAT SUCKED. SO KENNY IS YOUR MONEY BOY. HE WAS FUCKING FIRED UP LAST WEEK. YOU DID A GREAT JOB DICK! YOU DON'T EVEN KNOW YOUR OWN POWER! WAY TO DO IT DICK!

NO SHIT! MY FOLLOWER HAS RETURNED! WHO THE FUCK IS THAT WITH HIM?

"DICK! I AM A MEAT EATER! I DID IT! I GOT MARRIED THIS IS MY WIFE! I BROUGHT MY WIFE TO YOUR HOUSE! I DID IT DICK!"

"NO SHIT KENNY. FUCK. I AM PROUD OF YOU MAN! FUCK!"

OKAY MAN, YOU NEED TO CELEBRATE HIM. GO UP TO HIM! GIVE HIM A BIG ONE HAND BRO HUG THAT ALL THE GUYS ARE DOING NOW. HE REALLY FUCKING DID IT. FUCK. WHO IS THIS LADY? NO SHIT IT IS THE LADY THAT WORKS NIGHTS AT THE QUICKSTOP. THIS COULD BE A REAL THING. IT THINK SHE LIKED KENNY IN MIDDLE SCHOOL.

WHAT IF THIS IS A REAL WIFE AND HE IS NOT GOING TO BE A FUCK UP ANY MORE? WHAT IF HE IS GOING TO START TRYING TO TAKE OVER MY THRONE? YOU BETTER NOT LET HIM GROW TOO FAST DICK. HE COULD BE YOUR RIVAL! FUCK THAT GUY! HE IS EVIL!

"KENNY, WHO IS THIS LITTLE LADY?"

"SHE ISN'T ANY LITTLE LADY! SHE IS MY LITTLE LADY DICK! I DID IT! I DID IT! I AM A MEAT EATTER DICK! CAN YOU BELIEVE IT! I AIN'T NO FUCK UP NO MORE! I AM A MEAT EATTER!"

"KENNY, YEAH GREAT JOB! SETTLE DOWN. WHO IS THIS LADY STANDING ON MY LAWN??"

"OH RIGHT THIS IS MY WIFE BELINDA."

"WELL HELLO LADY. WHAT THE HELL ARE YOU DOING WITH THIS CRAZY ASS KENNY?"

"...hello...he.. he said we were meant to be together..."

"SHE IS THE ONE DICK! I DID IT!! YAHOOO!"

"WELL HOT DAMN! LETS DO THIS! KENNY YOU FUCKING DID IT! AND YOU BOUGHT HER A FUCKING RING MAN. WHERE DID YOU GET IT?"

"I SOLD ALL MY COMICS AND ALL THAT JEWELRY IN MY MA'S ROOM. FIGURED WHEN SHE CROAKS IT WOULD BE MINE ANYWAY. MIGHT AS WELL PUT IT TO USE NOW WHEN I NEED IT MOST!"

"FUCK KENNY YOU DID IT! NOW GO WITH YOUR LADY AND MAKE THAT BABY HAPPEN! THEN COME TO MY EVENT NEXT WEEK AT THE REC CENTER, YOU HEAR! YOU NEED TO BRING AT LEAST 10 PEOPLE! NOW YOU HAVE SEEN THE IMPACT OF THE F.A.T. A.S.S. METHOD HOW COULD YOU NOT SHARE IT AND SHARE IT AGAIN!"

"YES! YES! YES! I AM GOING TO BRING 20 PEOPLE!!! COM'ON WIFE! LETS GO!"

THE NEXT FRIDAY AT THE REC CENTER

HOLY SHIT DICK. YOU DID IT. IT IS YOUR FIRST REAL FUCKING MEAT-UP EVENT. IT IS LIKE THOSE PIECE OF SHITS ON TV DOING ALL THEIR FANCY SHIT. YOU ARE DOING BIG LEAGUE SHIT DICK. NO MORE JUST SITTING ON THE DAMN PORCH YELLING AT THOSE LAME ASS SACKS OF SHIT. IT IS GOING TO BE FUCKING AMAZING DICK. EVERYONE FOR GENERATIONS WILL KNOW YOUR NAME. THEY ARE GONNA MAKE BOOKS ABOUT YOU. SHIT THEY ARE GOING TO MAKE BOOKS ABOUT YOUR BOOKS! YOU FUCKING DID IT DICK!

FOLLOWERS GET READY FOR THE SHOW FOR YOUR LIVES!

WHERE ARE THEY...

I TOLD KENNY TO BE HERE AT 7 WHERE THE FUCK IS HE!

AND JIM AT WORK... I KNOW HE SAW FLIER. IT WAS ON THAT DAMN PRINTER PAPER ALL LAST WEEK. I KNOW HE SAW IT. HE BETTER DAMN SHOW UP.

IS THAT HIM. NO FUCKING SHIT ITS KENNY. YOU DID IT DICK! YOU MADE YOUR FIRST TRUE LEVEL 4 FOLLOWER. HOW MANY GOD DAMN PEOPLE DOES HE HAVE WITH HIM! HOT DOG! YOU ARE GOING TO BE RICH!

OKAY YOU GOT TO KEEP DRIVING HIM DICK! DON'T LET ON THAT YOU ARE PROUD OF HIM!

"KENNY YOU ARE LATE! WHAT THE FUCK KENNY! WHO ARE ALL THESE GREAT GUEST YOU HAVE HERE! WELCOME TO MEAT YOUR GOALS! I AM YOUR LEADER DICK HANDLER! COME SIT DOWN"

"DICK YOU ARE RIGHT I AM LATE! BUT I DID IT! I BROUGHT PEOPLE TO YOUR EVENT. LOOK THERE IS JIM

FROM YOUR WORK AND THE STEPHEN TWINS FROM ROUND THE CORNER. THEN MAMA. SEE MAMA CAME! MAMA WANTS TO BE A MEET EATER!"

"GREAT JOB KENNY! YOU ARE A MEAT EATER! YOU GET TO SIT AT THE FRONT OF THE ROOM NOW. NOW GET YOUR GUESTS ALL SEATED. HI MAMA, WELCOME! I KNEW YOU WOULD BE A MEAT EATER!"

"..hmmm... well you are getting that son of mine out of the house... so figured it may not be all made up...."

"YES MAM'! THIS IS THE REAL DEAL! HAVE A SEAT AND LETS GET STARTED!"

SO IT BEGINS DICK! YOU MADE IT! NOW JUST TELL THEM TO BUY YOUR SHIT!

MEAT LOG

YEAH OKAY! OKAY FOLLOWER!

ARE YOU READY TO BE A MEAT EATER FOR LIFE!!(TM)?

THERE IS NO POSSIBLE WAY YOU CAN SUCCEED BUT I LOVE LAUGHING AT YOUR ASS WHEN YOU FAIL, SO LETS DO THIS!

EACH WEEK WRITE IN YOUR NAME, DAY AND WHAT YOUR GOAL IS FOR THE WEEK!!

THEN AT THE END OF THE WEEK CHECK OFF IF YOU FAILED OR SUCCEEDED!

IF YOU SUCCEED YOU CAN BE A MEAT EATER FOR LIFE!!(TM)

I AM GIVING YOU YOUR LIFE!

I AM THE GREATEST!

I AM A MEAT EATER FOR LIFE!!(TM)

BUY MY SHIT!!!

I ASSFACE
_____

HAVE THE
AWESOMER
GOAL OF

DATE
_____

FAILURE
☒

DID-IT
☐

SOME
_____
BULLSHIT
_____

_____

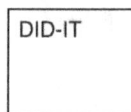

BY FRIDAY OR I AM
A LOSER AND
DON'T GET TO EAT
MEAT FOR A WEEK

I AM A MEAT EATER FOR LIFE!! (TM)

I _FART LICKER_____

HAVE THE ACTIONING GOAL OF

DATE
_____

FAILURE
❌

DID-IT
☐

_DOING JACK,_____

_SHIT_____

_____

BY FRIDAY OR I AM A LOSER AND DON'T GET TO EAT MEAT FOR A WEEK

I AM A MEAT EATER FOR LIFE!! (TM)

I ___YO MAMA_____

HAVE THE AWESOMER GOAL OF

DATE
_____

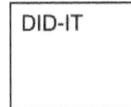

___WEARING_____

___BOOKERS AS_____

___EARINGS!_____

BY FRIDAY OR I AM A LOSER AND DON'T GET TO EAT MEAT FOR A WEEK

I AM A MEAT EATER FOR LIFE!! (TM)

I SHIT STREAK
_____

HAVE THE FUTUR-ISH GOAL OF

FAILURE
✗

DID-IT

WRITING A GOAL
_____
DOWN AND
_____
FORGETTING IT
_____

BY FRIDAY OR I AM A LOSER AND DON'T GET TO EAT MEAT FOR A WEEK

I AM A MEAT EATER FOR LIFE!! (TM)

I __TOILET SCUM__

HAVE THE SHAR-ED GOAL OF

DATE

FAILURE

✗

DID-IT

__TAKING A CRAP__

__AND BEING__

__PROUD OF IT__

BY FRIDAY OR I AM A LOSER AND DON'T GET TO EAT MEAT FOR A WEEK

I AM A MEAT EATER FOR LIFE!! (TM)

I __BUTT CRUST__

HAVE THE ACTIONING GOAL OF

THINKING I
AM BETTER
THAN YOU

BY FRIDAY OR I AM A LOSER AND DON'T GET TO EAT MEAT FOR A WEEK

I AM A MEAT EATER FOR LIFE!! (TM)

I _DUCHE GARGLER_

HAVE THE ACTIONING GOAL OF

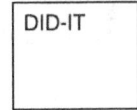

FLOSSING MY TEETH
WITH MY FINGER
NAIL CLIPING

BY FRIDAY OR I AM A LOSER AND DON'T GET TO EAT MEAT FOR A WEEK

I AM A MEAT EATER FOR LIFE!! (TM)

I LIBTARD
_____

HAVE THE
AWESOMER
GOAL OF

DATE
_____

FAILURE
✗

DID-IT

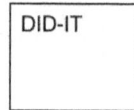

FLICKING 3
_____
BOOGERS UNDER
_____
THE COUCH
_____

BY FRIDAY OR I AM
A LOSER AND
DON'T GET TO EAT
MEAT FOR A WEEK

I AM A MEAT EATER FOR LIFE!! (TM)

I __TREE HUGGER__

HAVE THE AWESOMER GOAL OF

DATE
_____

FAILURE
✗

DID-IT

SMELLING AND BEING PROUD OF IT
_____
_____
_____

BY FRIDAY OR I AM A LOSER AND DON'T GET TO EAT MEAT FOR A WEEK

I AM A MEAT EATER FOR LIFE!! (TM)

I SCUM SUCKER
_____

HAVE THE AWESOMER GOAL OF

DATE
_____

FAILURE
✗

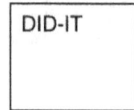

DID-IT

VOMMIT AND
_____

SWALLOW IT
_____

TWICE
_____

BY FRIDAY OR I AM A LOSER AND DON'T GET TO EAT MEAT FOR A WEEK

I AM A MEAT EATER FOR LIFE!! (TM)

I ___ASS FUNGUS_____

HAVE THE SHARED GOAL OF

DATE

_____

FAILURE
✕

DID-IT

___POPING A BLACK___
___HEAD AND___
___SHOWING IT OFF___

BY FRIDAY OR I AM A LOSER AND DON'T GET TO EAT MEAT FOR A WEEK

I AM A MEAT EATER FOR LIFE!! (TM)

I <u>MILIENIAL SHIT</u>

HAVE THE AWESOMER GOAL OF

DATE
_____

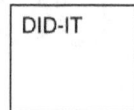

<u>DO NOTHING AND</u>

<u>BLAME MY</u>

<u>PARENTS FOR IT</u>

BY FRIDAY OR I AM A LOSER AND DON'T GET TO EAT MEAT FOR A WEEK

I AM A MEAT EATER FOR LIFE!! (TM)

I __TAILGATING FUCK__

HAVE THE AWESOMER GOAL OF

DATE
_____

FAILURE
✗

DID-IT

__CUSSING OUT__

__DUDES THEN__

__RUNNING AWAY__

BY FRIDAY OR I AM A LOSER AND DON'T GET TO EAT MEAT FOR A WEEK

I AM A MEAT EATER FOR LIFE!! (TM)

I SWEATY FART
_____

HAVE THE FUTURE-ISH GOAL OF

DATE
_____

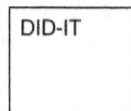

PAYING WITH EXACT
_____
FUCKING CHANGE,
_____
IN PENNIES
_____

BY FRIDAY OR I AM A LOSER AND DON'T GET TO EAT MEAT FOR A WEEK

I AM A MEAT EATER FOR LIFE!! (TM)

I __HIGH-PITCH ASS__

HAVE THE ACTIONING GOAL OF

DATE
_____

FAILURE
✗

DID-IT

__SAYING THE__
__MOST ANNYOING__
__SHIT EVER__

BY FRIDAY OR I AM A LOSER AND DON'T GET TO EAT MEAT FOR A WEEK

I AM A MEAT EATER FOR LIFE!! (TM)

I _FRANK_____

HAVE THE
AWESOMER
GOAL OF

DATE
_____

FAILURE
✗

DID-IT

HAVING MY SHIT
TOGETHER. FUCK
THAT GUY
_____

BY FRIDAY OR I AM
A LOSER AND
DON'T GET TO EAT
MEAT FOR A WEEK

I AM A MEAT EATER FOR LIFE!! (TM)

80

I ALARM CLOCK
_____

HAVE THE ACTIONING GOAL OF

_____

FAILURE
✗

DID-IT

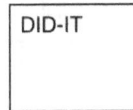

FUCKING UP THE
_____
BEST SEX DREAM
_____
EVER
_____

BY FRIDAY OR I AM A LOSER AND DON'T GET TO EAT MEAT FOR A WEEK

I AM A MEAT EATER FOR LIFE!! (TM)

I __DAVE__

HAVE THE
FUTURE-ISH
GOAL OF

DATE
DATE
___

FAILURE
×

DID-IT

LOOKING
_____
LIKE MY ASS
_____
FEELS
_____

BY FRIDAY OR I AM
A LOSER AND
DON'T GET TO EAT
MEAT FOR A WEEK

I AM A MEAT EATER FOR LIFE!! (TM)

I _FUCKIN' FUCKER_

HAVE THE AWESOMER GOAL OF

_____

FAILURE
✗

DID-IT

PRETENT TO
PICK UP MY
DOGS SHIT

BY FRIDAY OR I AM A LOSER AND DON'T GET TO EAT MEAT FOR A WEEK

I AM A MEAT EATER FOR LIFE!! (TM)

I __GUY NEXTDOOR__

HAVE THE ACTIONING GOAL OF

DATE
_____

FAILURE
☒

DID-IT

__LEAVING TRASH__
_____

__FUCKING__
_____

__EVERYWHERE__
_____

BY FRIDAY OR I AM A LOSER AND DON'T GET TO EAT MEAT FOR A WEEK

I AM A MEAT EATER FOR LIFE!! (TM)

I _MOTHER FUCKER_

HAVE THE AWESOMER GOAL OF

DATE
_____

FAILURE
✗

DID-IT

TAKE ALL THE
HOT SAUCE AT
THE WING PLACE

BY FRIDAY OR I AM A LOSER AND DON'T GET TO EAT MEAT FOR A WEEK

I AM A MEAT EATER FOR LIFE!! (TM)

SHIT THAT'S ON MY MIND

Dick here writing to you.

FOLLOWER.. you and I have been through some shit. I mean I am glad that I have never met you and will never have to hear you talk, but we have for sure been through some shit. And you paid me money, so you aren't totally worthless.

So because you don't wholly suck, I am going to tell it you it for real.

LIFE MOVES MAN... FUCK.... I KNOW I AM A GOD TO YOU. AND IN YOUR OATH AS A FOLLOWER YOU AGREED TO DO ANYTHING I SAY AND TO BRING MY NEWS PAPER TO MY FRONT PORCH ON SUNDAYS...

..but I am going to tell you.. life moves...

..god.. think about all that time when I was just sitting there..

..sitting on that damn stoop.. yelling at Ken... ..man that guy left town now and is making money making video games or some shit...

..what happened...   ...where are my kids...

DICK GET YOUR SHIT TOGETHER! YOU ARE ACTING LIKE ONE OF THOSE GOD DAMNED FOLLOWERS! THIS ISN'T THE FUCKING BOO-HOO LETS CRY LIKE A BABY SECTION... THIS IS THE SHIT THAT IS ON MY MIND SECTION..!!! GET A GRIP MAN!

YEAH! LETS GET BACK TO IT!

OKAY YEAH! SHIT THAT IS ON MY MIND!

FUCKING ALL THAT SHIT WITH THOSE GOD DAMNED LIBERALS TALKING A BUNCH OF BULLSHIT AND WHY THE FUCK, OH GOD, WHY THE FUCK IS MY TRUCK SO FUCKED??!

WHO FUCKED UP MY TRUCK??!!

WAS IT YOU!?!

I SEE YOU!!

I AM COMING FOR YOU MOTHER FUCKERS!

I AM A MEAT EATER FOR LIFE!!(TM)

BUY MY SHIT!!

BUY MY SHIT!

THAT'S RIGHT FOLLOWER!! IT IS TIME TO GET OUT YOUR MONEYS! AND.. SAY IT WITH ME..

BUY... MY... SHIT!!!

JUST COME EARLY TO THE MEAT-UP THIS FRIDAY AND BRING CASH!! NO FUCKING QUARTERS KENNY!

$7- My Official Shit from right after
Last Friday Nights first MEAT-UP!

$13 - The Official T-SHIRT That I
have been wearing for the past month.

$Free - The piss jug from my porch.
Half full.

www.ingramcontent.com/pod-product-compliance
Lightning Source LLC
Chambersburg PA
CBHW021135020426
42331CB00005B/782